WHEN THEY SAY...

OVERCOMING
BIAS
A PRACTICAL GUIDE FOR
DEVELOPING COGNITIVE CONTROL
OF UNCONSCIOUS BIAS

Andre Koen

Introduction

Bias Is Everywhere

Unconscious biases are prevalent in society and influence how we think, act, and interact with others. These biases form from societal norms and expectations and often operate subconsciously, making them difficult to recognize and challenge. Despite this, it is important to be aware of the role bias plays in our lives and work toward developing cognitive control over them. One effective way to do this is through cognitive behavioral therapy.

Unconscious bias and microaggressions are key concepts that can significantly impact individuals and organizations. Unconscious bias refers to the attitudes or stereotypes that affect our understanding, actions, and decisions in an unconscious manner (Moss-Racusin et al., 2014). Microaggressions are the subtle or indirect forms of discrimination experienced by individuals from marginalized groups (Sue et al., 2007).

Microaggressions are often behavioral expressions of unresolved unconscious bias. This chapter will explore the connection between unconscious bias and microaggressions, the cultural and contextual blind spots contributing to these phenomena, and how to overcome bias with cognitive-behavioral therapy tools.

Objectives

Bias Is Everywhere

Our goal is to raise awareness and understanding of unconscious bias and microaggressions and to provide practical tools and strategies to help readers overcome these issues in their personal and professional lives.

Key Objectives:

- We will discuss the cultural and contextual blind spots that can contribute to developing and perpetuating bias and microaggressions.

- We will then offer insights into how individuals can respond to microaggressions productively and constructively and how bystanders can intervene in situations involving microaggressions.

- Finally, we will examine the use of cognitive behavioral therapy tools to overcome bias, the role of self-awareness and mindfulness in addressing bias, and how organizations can promote a bias-aware culture.

Understanding Unconscious Bias & Microaggressions

Unconscious Bias and Cognitive Behavioral Therapy

As we grow and develop, we constantly form opinions and beliefs based on the experiences and information we encounter. Unfortunately, some of these opinions and beliefs can be biased, leading to harmful thoughts and actions toward others. This type of bias is known as unconscious bias, and it can be difficult to detect and overcome because it operates below the surface of our conscious awareness.

The good news is that there are methods for developing cognitive control that can help us overcome unconscious bias. One of these methods is cognitive behavioral therapy (CBT), a form of psychotherapy that effectively treats a range of psychological issues, including bias. CBT focuses on changing negative thought patterns and behaviors by addressing the underlying beliefs and assumptions that drive them.

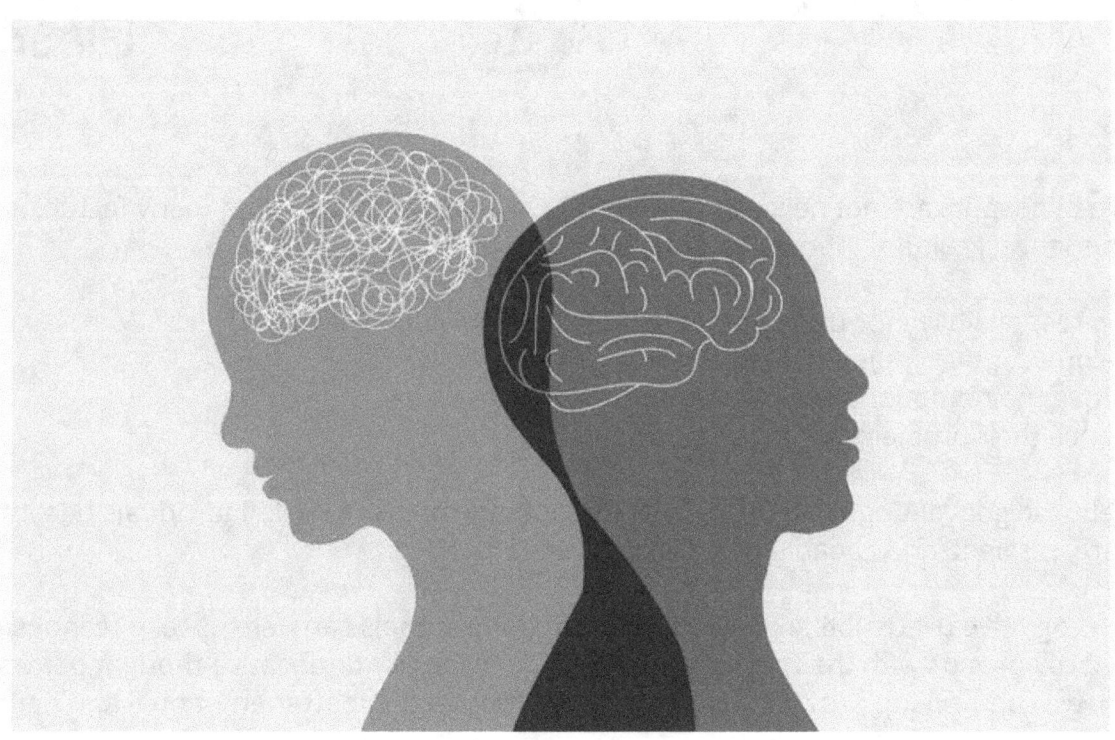

Unconscious Bias and Microaggressions

Unconscious bias and microaggressions are two key concepts that can significantly impact individuals and organizations. Unconscious bias refers to the attitudes or stereotypes that affect our understanding, actions, and decisions in an unconscious manner (Moss-Racusin et al., 2014). Microaggressions are the subtle or indirect forms of discrimination that can be experienced by individuals from marginalized groups (Sue et al., 2007).

Microaggressions are often behavioral expressions of unresolved unconscious bias. This chapter will explore the connection between unconscious bias and microaggressions, the cultural and contextual blind spots contributing to these phenomena, and how to overcome bias with cognitive-behavioral therapy tools.

Fault vs. Responsibility

Cognitive blindspots are not necessarily our fault, as they can result from many factors, such as past experiences, cultural influences, and cognitive biases.

By taking responsibility for our cognitive blindspots, individuals can:
- develop adaptive coping strategies,
- improve their emotional well-being, and
- enhance their problem-solving skills.

Ultimately, the goal of Cognitive Behavioral therapeutic tools is to help individuals become more self-aware, resilient, and capable of achieving their goals.

Although cognitive blindspots may not be our fault, these tools can help us take responsibility for them by providing us with the tools to identify and challenge our negative thought patterns. By doing so, we can develop positive ways of thinking that lead to better emotional and behavioral outcomes.

The connection between Unconscious Bias and Microaggressions:

Unconscious bias can contribute to the formation of microaggressions, as individuals may be unaware of their biases and the impact they have on others.

Microaggressions are often behavioral expressions of unresolved unconscious bias.

For example, a manager may unconsciously believe that women are less competent than men in leadership positions, leading them to overlook or undervalue the contributions of female team members. This could result in a microaggression episode, such as interrupting or dismissing their ideas in meetings (Moss-Racusin et al., 2014).

DO THIS...
What did you learn about others growing up?

If you learned about these social categories, place a check for each group and from what source.

Understanding Unconscious Bias and Microaggressions: Microaggressions are behavioral expressions of unresolved unconscious bias.

According to Sue (2010), microaggressions are "brief and commonplace daily verbal, behavioral, or environmental indignities, whether intentional or unintentional, that communicate hostile, derogatory, or negative slights and insults toward people from marginalized groups." In other words, microaggressions result from individuals' unconscious biases that may manifest in subtle forms of discrimination.

It is important to recognize that microaggressions can be unintentional and may stem from individuals' lack of awareness of their own biases (Nadal, 2011). Therefore, addressing unconscious bias can be an effective way to prevent and eliminate microaggressions. By increasing self-awareness and practicing mindfulness, individuals can identify their biases and take steps to address them (Greenwald & Banaji, 2013).

What did I learn? Plus + / Minus - / Zero 0

	African Americans	White Americans	Asian Americans	Native Americans	Disabled Americans	Latino/a Americans	LGBTQ Americans	Veteran Americans	Other Religions
Parents/Family									
Friends									
Workplace/ School									
TV/Movies & Media									
Personal Experience									

Unconscious Bias
Microaggression

Andre Koen copyright 2021

Common Forms of Unconscious Bias and Microaggressions

Here are three ways that microaggressions are tied to unresolved unconscious bias:

Stereotyping: Microaggressions often stem from stereotypes that individuals hold about certain groups. These stereotypes are often unconscious and can result in individuals making assumptions or judgments based on a person's identity, such as their race, gender, or sexual orientation. For example, assuming that all women are emotional or that all Asians are good at math.

Tokenism: Microaggressions can also be tied to tokenism, the practice of including individuals from underrepresented groups for the sake of appearance rather than genuine inclusivity. Individuals who engage in tokenism may believe they are being inclusive, but their actions may be rooted in unconscious biases or prejudices.

Bias in Decision-Making: Unconscious bias can also influence decision-making in the workplace, such as hiring, promotions, and performance evaluations. For example, an individual may unconsciously rate women lower on leadership skills than men with the same qualifications or select candidates with similar backgrounds or experiences.

These biases can result in microaggressions that further perpetuate inequities in the workplace.

The Research

Overall, it is essential to understand the connection between unconscious bias and microaggressions and to take steps to address these issues to promote a more inclusive and equitable society.

Research has shown that unconscious biases are often automatic and can be influenced by cultural and contextual factors (Greenwald & Banaji, 2013). These biases can lead to microaggressions, which can have a harmful impact on the targeted individuals or groups (Nadal, 2011). For instance, microaggressions can result in lower self-esteem, negative affect, and stress for the individuals targeted by these behaviors (Sue et al., 2007).

Things to think about:

What is unconscious bias and how does it develop?

....

....

How does unconscious bias affect our thoughts, feelings, and behavior?

....

....

What are some common forms of unconscious bias?

....

....

Things to do:

- Take an online Implicit Association Test (IAT) to assess your own unconscious biases
- Reflect on how your unconscious biases may impact your personal and professional relationships
- Seek out resources (books, articles, podcasts, etc.) to learn more about unconscious bias and its effects

Notes

....

....

....

Microaggressions

Things to think about:

What are microaggressions and how do they differ from overt forms of discrimination?

....
....
....

What are some common examples of microaggressions?

....
....
....

How do microaggressions impact individuals and groups?

....
....
....

Things to do:

- Reflect on times when you may have witnessed or perpetuated microaggressions, and consider how you could have responded differently.

- Research strategies for addressing and preventing microaggressions in personal and professional settings

- Practice active listening and empathy to understand better the experiences of individuals targeted with microaggressions.

Notes

....
....
....
....

Cultural and Contextual Blind Spots

Cultural and contextual blind spots can also contribute to unconscious bias and microaggressions. Blind spots can occur when individuals are unaware of their biases or the cultural contexts in which they operate. For example, an individual may be unaware of the stereotypes and biases that are prevalent in their organization or industry. They may also need to be made aware of the historical and systemic factors that contribute to the experiences of marginalized groups.

Cultural and Contextual Blind Spots

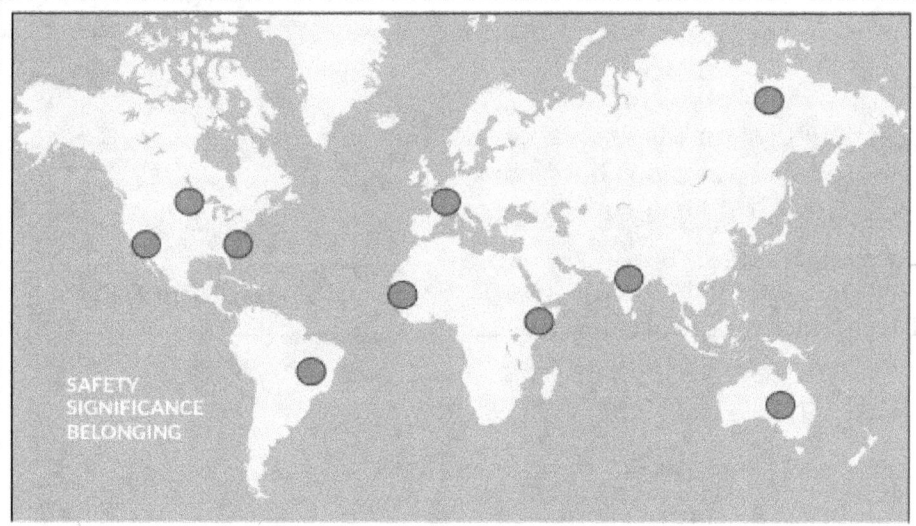

Cultural and contextual blind spots can contribute to the formation of unconscious biases and the perpetuation of microaggressions.

How might your geographic region impact you cultural norms or tradition?

....

....

How might geographic regions impact other's cultural norms or tradition?

....

....

....

....

Cultural and Contextual Blind Spots

Here are a few ways our cultural context and geographic regions can shape our worldview and complicate our human relationships. At our core, we have our values, but what they mean and how they are each secured are often very different.

- **Socialization:** The context and geography in which an individual is raised can shape their perceptions and attitudes towards different groups of people. For example, individuals who grow up in a homogeneous community may be less exposed to people from different backgrounds, leading to a lack of understanding or awareness of other cultures. This can result in unconscious biases towards those groups.

- **Cultural Norms:** Cultural norms and values can also contribute to unconscious bias. For example, some cultures may value conformity and uniformity, resulting in negative attitudes toward those who deviate from the norm. Similarly, cultural attitudes towards gender, race, and other identity categories can also influence unconscious biases towards those groups.

- **Systemic Inequality:** The context and geography of an individual's community can also contribute to systemic inequality, which can, in turn, perpetuate unconscious bias. For example, racially or socioeconomically segregated communities may lead to disparities in access to resources and opportunities, which can create unconscious biases towards certain groups based on their perceived level of success or achievement.

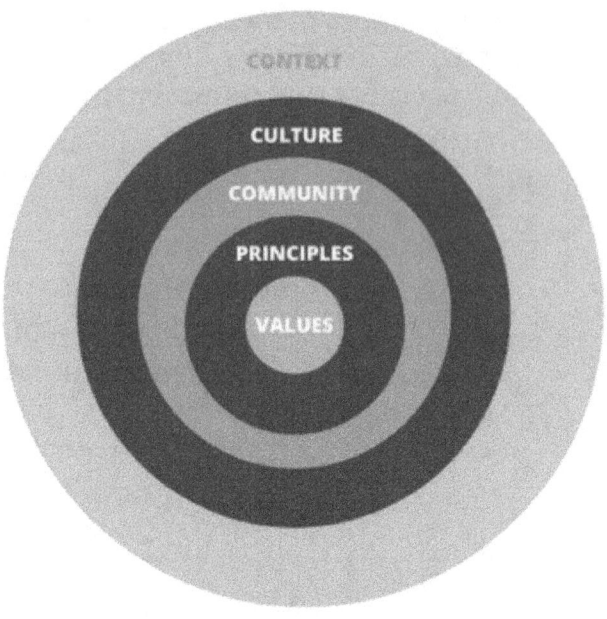

By increasing awareness and understanding of how context and geography can shape biases, individuals can take proactive steps to mitigate their impact, such as seeking out diverse perspectives, educating themselves on different cultures and experiences, and actively challenging biases in themselves and others.

Things to think about:

How can geography impact customs, food choices, art, or interpersonal relationships?

Can you think of a tradition that is rooted in a place-based culture?

Describe a "Folk Food" and share a story about it.

What impact might your ancestral home have on the way people communicate today?

What role does geography play in the creation of a worldview?

Things to do:

- Learn more about your culture to understand your people's historical significance better.

- Engage in self-reflection and seek education and training to increase awareness of other cultural groups.

- Advocate for policies and practices that promote diversity, equity, and inclusion in organizations.

Creating Greater Cognitive Control

In the context of overcoming bias, CBT can involve identifying and challenging negative thoughts and beliefs about different groups of people. This can include exploring the evidence for and against these thoughts and learning to view people from different backgrounds with empathy and respect. CBT can also involve developing new habits and practices that counteract our unconscious biases and help us treat all people with dignity and respect.

The Cognitive Behavioral Therapy (CBT) diagram.
There are three interconnected components - thoughts, feelings, and behaviors - which are interrelated and can cyclically influence each other.
This diagram demonstrates the connections of how each can influence feelings and behaviors and that behaviors can be either adaptive or maladaptive.

Adaptive in this context refers to the ability to achieve goals.

Maladaptive is a behavior that does not achieve goals.

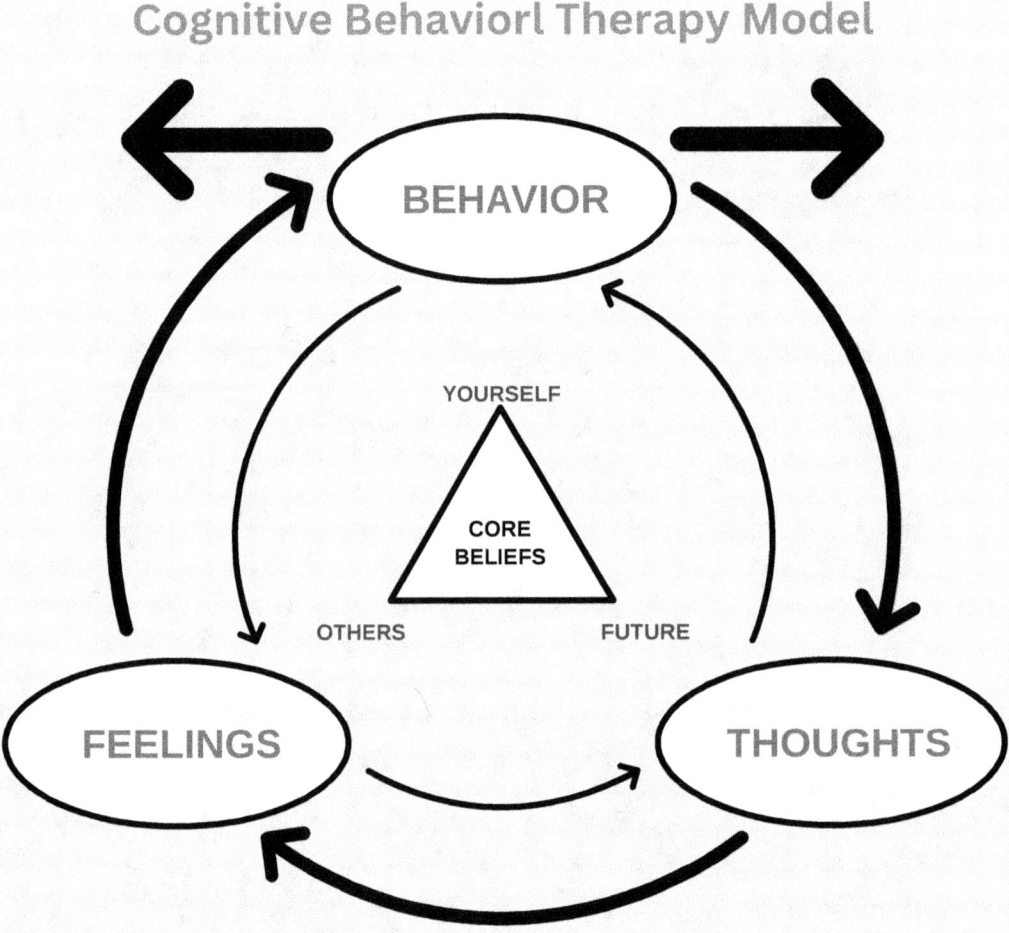

Cognitive Behaviorl Therapy Model

Creating Greater Cognitive Control

To create better cognitive controls over microaggressions and unconscious bias, cognitive-behavioral therapy (CBT) tools can be utilized. CBT aims to modify negative thinking patterns and maladaptive behaviors by increasing awareness, self-monitoring, and challenging negative thoughts (Beck, 2011). The following are some ways to use CBT tools to address unconscious bias and prevent microaggressions:

Identify and Challenge Negative Thoughts: Individuals can learn to identify negative thoughts that may stem from their unconscious biases and challenge them using evidence-based techniques (Beck, 2011). For instance, individuals can ask themselves, "What evidence do I have to support this negative thought?" or "Is there another way to interpret this situation?"

Practice Mindfulness: Mindfulness can help individuals increase their awareness of their thoughts, feelings, and bodily sensations. Which can, in turn, increase their ability to recognize and control their unconscious biases (Segal, Williams, & Teasdale, 2002). Mindfulness practices such as meditation or deep breathing exercises can increase present-moment awareness.

Increase Exposure to Diverse Perspectives: Individuals can seek out and expose themselves to diverse perspectives to challenge their unconscious biases (Dovidio et al., 2015). For instance, individuals can read books or watch documentaries that feature stories and perspectives of marginalized groups.

By utilizing CBT tools, individuals can increase their self-awareness and develop strategies to address their unconscious biases, ultimately reducing microaggressions and creating a more inclusive society.

How do you think CBT can help individuals gain greater cognitive control?

What are some techniques used in CBT that can help individuals to gain great cognitive control over biases?

Can you think of a situation where it might be important to recognize and manage a bias?

How do you think becoming more self-aware and reducing the impact of our biases can help us create a more inclusive and respectful environment?

How do you think we can encourage others?

Notes

Overcoming Bias with Cognitive Behavioral Therapy Tools

Cognitive Restructuring

One technique used in CBT is cognitive restructuring, which involves identifying and challenging automatic negative thoughts and replacing them with more balanced and positive thoughts (Beck, 1979). For example, if an individual has the automatic thought that members of a certain race are inherently lazy, they can challenge that thought by examining evidence to the contrary and replacing it with a more accurate and balanced thought, such as acknowledging that there are hardworking individuals of all races.

Cognitive Distortions

Another technique used in CBT is identifying and addressing cognitive distortions, which are common thinking errors that can contribute to biased attitudes and behaviors (Beck, 1979). Some common cognitive distortions include black-and-white thinking, jumping to conclusions, and overgeneralizing. By becoming aware of these distortions and learning to challenge them, individuals can reduce the impact of unconscious biases on their thoughts and behaviors.

CBT can also help individuals develop skills such as perspective-taking and empathy, which can increase understanding and reduce biased attitudes and behaviors (Ecklund et al., 2016).

Overcoming Bias with Cognitive Behavioral Therapy Tools

Leaders can promote empathy and perspective-taking by encouraging individuals to challenge their own biases and assumptions. This can involve identifying and questioning negative thoughts or beliefs about different racial groups and actively seeking information and experiences that challenge these biases.

Here are three steps that can help individuals increase empathy and perspective-taking:

- **Practice Active Listening:** Active listening involves paying close attention to what someone is saying and trying to understand their perspective without judgment or interruption. This can include asking open-ended questions, paraphrasing what the person has said to ensure understanding, and reflecting on your own reactions and biases.

- **Seek Out Diverse Perspectives:** To increase empathy and perspective-taking, it's vital to seek out diverse perspectives and experiences. This can involve exposing yourself to different cultures, beliefs, and experiences through reading, traveling, or talking to people from different backgrounds. You can broaden your understanding and become more empathetic toward others by actively seeking diverse perspectives.

- **Challenge Your Assumptions:** Finally, to increase empathy and perspective-taking, it's important to challenge your own assumptions and biases. This can involve actively questioning your beliefs, considering alternative perspectives, and seeking feedback from others. By taking an honest and reflective approach to your biases, you can become more aware of how they may influence your thinking and behavior and work to address them more positively and productively.

Cognitive Distortions and Cognitive Restructuring

👆 **Things to think about:**

What are cognitive distortions, and how do they relate to bias and microaggressions?

....

....

....

What are some common examples of cognitive distortions related to bias?

....

....

....

How can cognitive restructuring be used to address bias and reduce the likelihood of microaggressions?

....

....

....

🧠 **Things to do:**

- Identify and reflect on your own cognitive distortions related to bias, and work on challenging and reframing them

- Seek out professional support (such as a therapist) to address deeply ingrained biases or cognitive distortions.

- Practice mindfulness and self-reflection to become more aware of your thoughts and biases in the moment.

Notes

....

....

....

....

Interventions

There are a variety of behavioral interventions that can help address bias and microaggressions. For example, implicit bias training programs can help people become more aware of their biases and learn strategies to reduce that impact on their behavior. Additionally, bystander intervention training can teach individuals how to intervene when they witness microaggressions or other forms of bias.

- How can organizations ensure that their policies and practices effectively address and prevent microaggressions?

- How can individuals continue to educate themselves and stay updated on best practices for addressing bias and microaggressions in their personal and professional lives?

While changing individual attitudes and beliefs is important in addressing bias and microaggressions, interventions focusing solely on individual-level changes are often insufficient. Changing the broader social and cultural context in which these behaviors occur is also necessary. This involves addressing larger systems of power and privilege and creating more inclusive policies and practices in organizations.

 Things to do:

- Advocate for and participate in bystander intervention training in your workplace or community.

- Review your organization's policies and procedures to identify potential areas for improvement in addressing and preventing microaggressions.

- Educate yourself on the latest research and best practices for addressing bias and microaggressions, and share this information with your colleagues and friends.

Behavioral Interventions

 Things to think about:

What are behavioral interventions, and how do they relate to bias and microaggressions?

What are some common examples of behavioral interventions that can address bias and reduce the likelihood of microaggressions?

How can behavioral interventions be implemented in personal and professional settings?

Things to do:

- Identify situations in which you may be prone to bias or microaggressions, and plan specific behavioral interventions to avoid or mitigate them.

- Seek out training or support to develop and implement effective behavioral interventions.

- Reflect on the impact of your behavioral interventions and adjust them as necessary.

Things to think about:

What is empathy, and how does it relate to bias and microaggressions?

What are some common barriers to empathy and perspective-taking, and how can they be overcome?

Organizations can implement policies and practices that address and prevent microaggressions. This can include conducting regular diversity, equity, and inclusion training for all employees, implementing policies that explicitly prohibit microaggressions, and creating mechanisms for reporting and addressing instances of microaggressions.

Things to think about:

How many triangles do you see?

What if there were none at all?

Increasing Empathy and Perspective-Taking

In 1955, Joseph Luft and Harrington Ingham created the Johari window model. The model is named after a combination of their first names (Jo-seph and Har-ington). Luft and Ingham were American psychologists who developed the Johari window as a tool to help individuals and groups improve their self-awareness and communication skills.

Johari's Window

Johari's window can be an effective tool for creating more self-awareness and communication. Organizations can improve teamwork, decision-making, and overall success by promoting open communication and self-reflection.

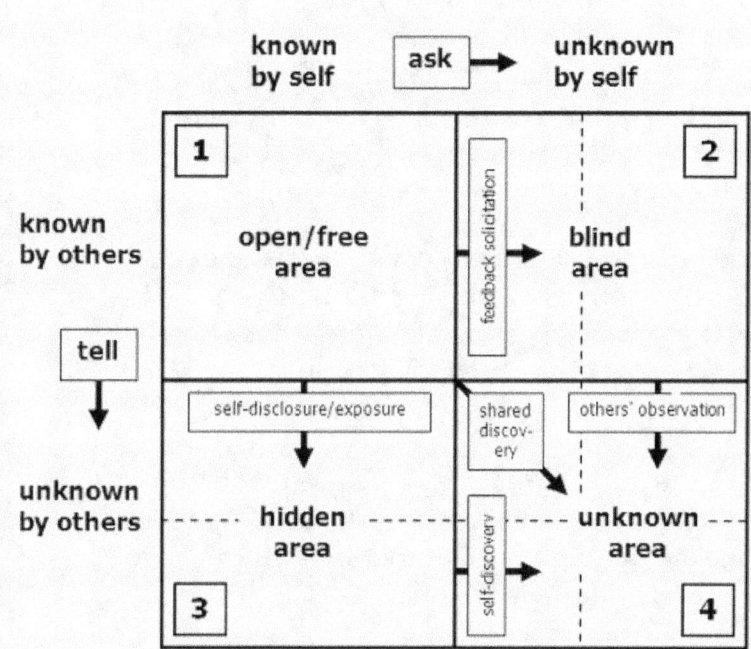

Using Johari's Window to Examine and Overcome Bias

Bias can be a difficult thing to understand and overcome. However, one tool that can be helpful in this process is the Johari Window. The Johari Window is a model for understanding self-awareness and communication between individuals. It has four quadrants, each representing a different aspect of self-awareness.

The first quadrant is the "Open Self." This quadrant represents information about ourselves that we are aware of and that others are aware of. The second quadrant is the "Hidden Self." This quadrant represents information about ourselves that we know, but others do not. The third quadrant is the "Blind Self." This quadrant represents information about ourselves that we are unaware of but that others are.

Finally, the fourth quadrant is the "Unknown Self." This quadrant represents information about ourselves that neither we nor others know.

To overcome bias, it is crucial to understand what is in each quadrant of our Johari Window. By examining the "Blind Self," we can learn about the biases and assumptions that we hold without even realizing it. By exploring the "Hidden Self," we can understand why we have these biases and how they may affect our interactions with others.

One way to use the Johari Window to overcome bias is to solicit feedback from others. By asking people we trust to share their perceptions of us, we can gain insight into what is in our "Blind Self" and "Hidden Self." We can then work on challenging and changing these biases consciously.

Another way to use the Johari Window is to engage in self-reflection. By examining our thoughts, beliefs, and actions, we can gain insight into what is in our "Hidden Self." We can then work to change these biases through conscious effort and education.

Overall, the Johari Window can be a valuable tool in overcoming bias. By increasing our self-awareness and seeking feedback from others, we can work to understand and challenge our biases.

Things to think about:

What aspect of the Johari Window can help be more effective in creating a more diverse organization?

What is the purpose of examining the "Blind Self" and "Hidden Self" in the Johari Window?

How can soliciting feedback from others be used to overcome bias?

How can self-reflection help us to overcome our biases?

In what ways can the Johari Window be useful in the process of overcoming bias?

Conclusion

As mentioned earlier, microaggressions are often connected to unconscious bias. Our unconscious biases can influence how we treat people and the microaggressions we may commit. It's important to understand that unconscious bias does not necessarily reflect a person's moral character; instead, it results from societal messages and cultural norms we have internalized over time.

It's possible to challenge and overcome unconscious bias through self-reflection and self-awareness. By examining our biases, we can better understand how they influence our behavior and work to change them. This can involve seeking out diverse perspectives, challenging our assumptions, and being mindful of our thoughts and actions in our daily lives.

Addressing bias and microaggressions is an ongoing process requiring individual and systemic change. Through developing a better understanding of unconscious bias, microaggressions, and the cultural and contextual blind spots that contribute to them, we can begin to take steps to create more inclusive environments in our personal and professional lives. Using cognitive-behavioral therapy tools and behavioral interventions, we can learn to recognize and overcome our biases and work towards building a more equitable and just society.

What new insights or information did you gain from this chapter, and how will you apply it in your personal and professional life?

What additional steps can organizations take to address and prevent microaggressions beyond those discussed in this chapter?

How can we continue to push for more significant systemic change to address bias and microaggressions at a broader level?

Notes

Bibliography

Beck, J. S. (2011). Cognitive behavior therapy: Basics and beyond. Guilford Press.

Dovidio, J. F., Love, A., Schellhaas, F. M. H., & Hewstone, M. (2015). Reducing intergroup bias through intergroup contact: Twenty years of progress and future directions. Group Processes & Intergroup Relations, 18(3), 356-376.

Segal, Z. V., Williams, J. M., & Teasdale, J. D. (2002). Mindfulness-based cognitive therapy for depression: A new approach to preventing relapse. Guilford Press.

American Psychological Association. (2020). Unconscious Bias. Retrieved from https://www.apa.org/ed/governance/division-17/resources/unconscious-bias

Cokley, K. (2017). A Critical Review of the Research on Microaggressions in Psychology. Race and Social Problems, 9(2), 101-125.

Dovidio, J. F., Gaertner, S. L., & Saguy, T. (2018). Another View of "We Are All Racists Now": Race and Response to National Events. Journal of Social Issues, 74(1), 15-39.

Greenwald, A. G., & Krieger, L. H. (2006). Implicit bias: Scientific foundations. California Law Review, 94(4), 945-967.

Nelson, T. D. (2005). Ageism: Prejudice against our feared future self. Journal of Social Issues, 61(2), 207-221.

Sue, D. W., Capodilupo, C. M., Torino, G. C., Bucceri, J. M., Holder, A. M. B., Nadal, K. L., & Esquilin, M. (2007). Racial microaggressions in everyday life: Implications for clinical practice. American Psychologist, 62(4), 271-286.

Trawalter, S., Hoffman, K. M., & Waytz, A. (2015). Racial bias in perceptions of others' pain. PLoS One, 10(11), e0143836.

DIVERSITY, EQUITY & INCLUSION

Andre Koen

Andre Koen is a speaker, consultant, and educator specializing in diversity, equity, and inclusion. He is the founder and president of AM Horizons, a consulting firm that provides services to organizations looking to create a more equitable and inclusive environment.

Koen has worked with various clients, including educational institutions, government agencies, and nonprofit organizations.

He has over 25 years of experience in the field and has received numerous awards for his work.

He is known for his engaging and thought-provoking presentations, which challenge audiences to think critically about issues related to diversity and inclusion.

ANDRE KOEN

SHIFTING PARADIGMS
ENKINDLING MINDS

Andre Koen ///// 651-998-9376 ///// andrekoen.com ///// amkeok@gmail.com DIVERSITY/EQUITY/INCLUSION/BELONGING

OVERCOMING
BIAS
A PRACTICAL GUIDE FOR
DEVELOPING COGNITIVE CONTROL
OF UNCONSCIOUS BIAS.

Andre Koen